How to Use Your Interactive Storybook & Story Buddy™:

1. Activate your Story Buddy™ by pressing the "On / Off" button on the ear.
2. Read the story aloud in a quiet place. Speak in a clear voice when you see the highlighted phrases.
3. Listen to your Story Buddy™ respond with several different phrases throughout the book.

Clarity and speed of reading affect the way Bigsby™ responds. He may not always respond to young children.

Watch for even more Interactive Storybooks & Story Buddy™ characters. For more information, visit us on the Web at www.Hallmark.com/StoryBuddy.

Copyright © 2011 Hallmark Licensing, Inc.

Published by Hallmark Gift Books,
a division of Hallmark Cards, Inc.,
Kansas City, MO 64141
Visit us on the Web at www.Hallmark.com.

Editor: Emily Osborn
Art Director: Kevin Swanson
Designer: Scott Swanson
Production Artist: Bryan Ring

ISBN: 978-1-59530-370-7
KOB8027

Printed and bound in China
JUL 11

BOOK 3

BIGSBY'S
Big News

Hallmark
GIFT BOOKS

**Written by Jake Gahr . Illustrated by Bob Kolar
Character & Concept by Scott Swanson**

No one knew about giant, furry Bigsby except
his best friends, Sam and June. It was summertime,
and the three friends were having tons of fun
playing in the forest. They had mud-ball fights,
played tag, juggled, joked, and danced.

They also swam and splashed in the pond a lot.
Bigsby couldn't get enough of the water.

Someone else was in the forest a lot that summer, too. Sam's neighbor, Mr. Jasper, spent all day in the woods trying to get proof that Bigsby was real.

He searched every nook and cranny (even though Bigsby was much too big to fit in a cranny) until...

Click! Bigsby felt a shiver up his back.

Sam and June decided to walk into town. They wanted to see just how bad the "big news" might be.

"Flyin' flapjacks!" Sam yelped. There were people all over town, too.

"Sam," June said, "Bigsby can't hide forever. We have to figure out how to stop all this!"

Sam and June had a great and tricky idea. If they made people think that Mr. Jasper's picture was a fake, then maybe everyone would quit looking for the real Bigsby!

But Sam and June weren't big enough to do it alone. They'd need help...big time.

The three friends would build giant look-alike furry
creatures for people to find so they'd stop looking for the
real one. Everything would go back to normal.

Back in the forest, they measured the real Bigsby, which
took awhile because Bigsby was very, very ticklish.

After that, they searched the forest and their houses for stuff to use to build the look-alikes. By the time they were done, they had three Bigsby decoys that looked so much like Bigsby, the plan was sure to work! Bigsby thought his buddies were the greatest.

They put the first look-alike next to the tallest tree in the forest. Even though it wasn't a real Bigsby, people were excited to find him, anyway.

Not Mr. Jasper, though. When he saw the look-alike creature, he was a little confused.

The day after that, the second look-alike was found "swimming" in the pond. It looked like it was having so much fun! The real Bigsby wanted to run out and dive in, too! Bigsby couldn't get enough of the water.

Early the next morning, the third
look-alike was found. It was doing
a little "window shopping" right
in the middle of Main Street.
   "I wonder if they have a shirt
in Bigsby's size," Sam joked.
The friends thought it was
very funny.

By the time the afternoon paper came out, the excitement was all over. The news of the Bigsby decoys had spread through town. The people who lived there went back inside. The people who didn't went back to wherever they were from.

Sam and June's plan had worked, which was great, because now Bigsby really wanted to play.

That's just what the three friends were doing when Mr. Jasper bumped into them on his way home! First, Mr. Jasper thought Bigsby was a tree. Then he thought Bigsby was another look-alike creature. Then he thought, "It's HIM! He's real! And my camera's at HOOOOME!" Bigsby smiled nervously, and waved.

As Mr. Jasper ran off to get his camera, Sam and June hugged their giant furry friend. He was not a look-alike or a tree. Bigsby was real. Together Sam and June said, "You're the best friend a kid could ever have!"

Did you have fun reading with Bigsby™? We would love to hear from you!

Please send your comments to:
Hallmark Book Feedback
P.O. Box 419034
Mail Drop 215
Kansas City, MO 64141

Or e-mail us at:
booknotes@hallmark.com

BIGSBY TIMBER CO.
"We cut 'em all the way down!"

S	M	T	W	T	F	S
			1	2	3	4
						5
6	7	8	9	10	11	12
13	14	15	16	17	18	19
20	21	22	23	24	25	26
27	28	29	30			

Found a footprint on the mushroom ridge trail

seen him by Ruby creek!